I Am a
GORILLA

Level 2

Written by Lori C. Froeb

Silver Dolphin

P1 **PRE-LEVEL 1: ASPIRING READERS**

 1 **LEVEL 1: EARLY READERS**

 2 **LEVEL 2: DEVELOPING READERS**

- Simple factual texts with mostly familiar themes and content
- Concepts in text are supported by images
- Includes glossary to reinforce reading comprehension
- Repetition of basic sentence structure with variation of placement of subjects, verbs, and adjectives
- Introduction to new phonic structures
- Integration of contractions, possessives, compound sentences, and some three-syllable words
- Mostly easy vocabulary familiar to kindergarteners and first-graders

 3 **LEVEL 3: ENGAGED READERS**

 4 **LEVEL 4: FLUENT READERS**

Silver Dolphin Books
An imprint of Printers Row Publishing Group
A division of Readerlink Distribution Services, LLC
10350 Barnes Canyon Road, Suite 100, San Diego, CA 92121
www.silverdolphinbooks.com

ISBN: 978-1-68412-870-9
Manufactured, printed, and assembled in Guangzhou, China.
First printing, October 2019. GD/10/19
23 22 21 20 19 1 2 3 4 5

Hello! Welcome to Africa.

I am a gorilla.

There are two **species** of gorillas.

Western gorillas live in rain forests and marshes in western Africa.

They live in Cameroon, Gabon, and a few other countries.

western gorilla

AFRICA

eastern gorilla

Eastern gorillas live in mountain forests in parts of central Africa.

They are found in Rwanda, Uganda, and the Congo.

I am an eastern gorilla.

Gorillas are great apes.

Bonobos, orangutans, and chimpanzees are also great apes.

Apes do not have tails like monkeys do.

gorilla
largest of the apes

bonobo
most peaceful of the apes

Monkey, not an ape!

Monkeys have tails. Apes do not.

orangutan

spends most of its life in trees

chimpanzee

closest **relative** to humans

Most apes live in Africa just like me!

Orangutans live in Asia.

Look at me. Do you think you and I look a little alike?

Humans, gorillas, and all apes are **primates**.

Monkeys are primates, too.

Primates have big brains and eyes that face forward.

Primates also have long fingers and toes.

Most primates have **opposable thumbs**.

This means we can use our thumbs to grasp things.

Humans and gorillas share more than ninety-six percent of their DNA.

DNA is what makes us what we are. It is in all our cells.

No wonder we look a little alike!

You are part of a family. I am part of a family, too.

My mom and I are part of a **troop**. A troop is a group of gorillas.

We do everything together.

My dad is in charge of the troop. He is a silverback.

The hair on his back turned silver when he became a teenager.

When I get older, I will be a silverback, too.

Dad makes sure our troop is safe.

He decides where we look for food.

If there is a fight in the troop, Dad breaks it up.

Gorillas are peaceful apes.

Most times there are no fights.

But Dad is always on the lookout for trouble.

If he sees a male gorilla he does not know, he may roar.

Sometimes he will beat his chest.

The other gorilla knows this means, "I am in charge."

Gorillas do not have many predators.

But our numbers in the wild are shrinking.

Humans are the biggest danger to gorillas.

Humans hunt and capture gorillas.

They also destroy gorilla **habitats**.

Today, all gorillas are **endangered**.

Gorillas use twenty-five sounds to **communicate**.

We can scream if we are angry or scared.

We hum when we eat.

A hum means we are happy.

A mother gorilla can make a grunting sound like a pig.

She uses this to tell her baby he is doing something wrong.

All gorillas walk using their knuckles and legs.

This would be very hard for you to do.

It is easy for us.

Our arms are very strong and much longer than our legs.

We can stand and walk on our feet, too.

This is helpful when we are carrying food.

Speaking of food, it is time to look for some with my troop.

Eastern gorillas are **herbivores**.

We **forage** for many hours every day.

We spend all morning looking for food. Then we nap.

When we wake up, we forage for the rest of the day.

Western gorillas are also mainly herbivores.

Fruit is easy to find in their forest, so they eat a lot of it.

They eat more than one hundred different kinds of fruit!

If fruit is hard to find, these gorillas eat leaves and bark.

Some also like to eat ants and termites.

ant

bark

leaves

termite

A hungry western gorilla may look for a termite nest.

He breaks the nest to get at the juicy termites inside.

All this foraging and eating has made me sleepy.

My troop gets ready to nap by building nests.

Mom finds branches and leaves.

She makes a nest for us on the ground.

We make a new nest every time we sleep.

I am learning how to make a nest from my mom.

After naptime, I like to play with my friends.

We climb trees, swing from branches, and wrestle.

Sometimes we even play tag!

Gorillas learn from playing.

We learn how to get along with others in our group.

We also learn how to use our arms to swing.

My friends are calling me to play right now.

See you later!

Gorillas Are Great!

An adult gorilla can eat sixty pounds of food a day!

A baby gorilla can ride on its mother's back when it is four months old. It holds on tightly.

A gorilla nose print is like a human fingerprint. No two are exactly alike!

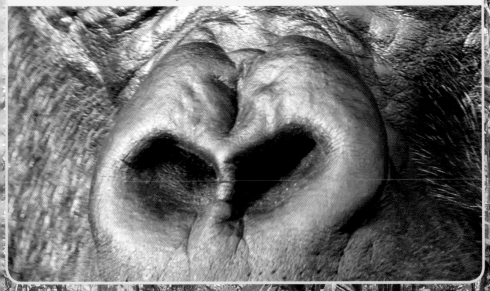

Gorillas get the water they need from plants they eat.

Glossary

communicate: to share information, ideas, and feelings

endangered: almost none left in the world

forage: to look around for food

habitat: the place where an animal lives

herbivore: an animal that eats only plants

opposable thumbs: thumbs that can be used to grasp and hold things

primate: a type of mammal that has hands that can grasp, forward-facing eyes, and large brains for their size

relative: someone who came from the same ancestor

species: a group of living things different from all other groups

troop: a group of gorillas